If You Were a Teacher

by Fay Robinson
illustrated by
Shelley Dieterichs

MODERN CURRICULUM PRESS

Pearson Learning Group

If you were a teacher, you could never be late to school. You'd promise to get there before any children arrived.

You'd say "hi" to the teacher in the next room.

Then you'd hurry to set things up.
You'd be glad to see all the children
as they came in.

3

In the morning, you might teach reading. You'd know just how to do it. (You had to learn how in college!)

You'd keep track of what each child needs to learn. You'd know that Max needs help with silent letters. And Sue knows them all.

You'd teach writing too. You might
have students write about a bear that left
the forest to live in the city.

If you were a teacher, you'd line children up for gym. They might be noisy. Then you'd flick the lights to get their attention.

While your class was at gym, you'd have lots to do. You'd check workbooks. You'd start to read your students' bear stories. Just when you got comfortable, a bell would ring. Gym class would be over already.

If you were a teacher, you'd teach
math. (You learned that in college too.)

To show three times two, you would
hand out pears. Three children could hold
two pears each. But somebody might
drop his or hers.

Then you'd have a clean-up problem,
not a math problem.

At lunch time, you'd eat in the teacher's room. Or you'd eat with your class. Either way, you'd feel comfortable.

After lunch, maybe you'd talk about bones. You'd use a model. You got it at a store for teachers.

You'd know all the bones are there.
You counted them twice last night. (And
you took out a chicken bone. How did
that get there?)

If you were a teacher, you could read at the end of the day. You'd pick your favorite book. You'd hope the children like it as much as you do.

After school, the class would go home. But you'd have lots more to do. You might meet with Max's mom. You'd promise to help Max with reading.

You'd check to see who circled the
right answers in math. And you'd finish
reading your students' stories.

You'd go home long after the kids left. You'd be very tired. But if you were a teacher, you wouldn't mind. You'd really like helping children learn. So it would all be worth it!